Share My Gold

ISBN: 1463722451
ISBN-13: 9781463722456

OTHER BOOKS BY DOLLY YATES

Tales From the Teapot

One Heart Two Countries

Can be purchased by:

dollyyates@yahoo.com
www.amazon.com
www.createspace.com/3652836
and other retailers

Share My Gold

BY

DOLLY YATES

Dedication

I dedicate this book in memory of my mother,
Georgina Robson who brought me to discover
Christ as my Lord and Saviour.

About the Book

The author sees her life as a gold-miner discovering nuggets of gold when least expected. She opens up by describing how she found her "mother lode" the day when the Lord became real to her at a young age.

Sometimes her life experiences have become nuggets of gold as the Lord gave her the insight through scripture to overcome her fears and anxieties. Other times everyday things have become nuggets of gold as she perceived spiritual truths hidden there.

Often the author's nuggets have popped straight out of God's Word as light from the scriptures entered her heart in a new understanding.

Even as the book comes to a close you are left with the anticipation that there is ever more and more nuggets of gold just waiting to be discovered.

Acknowledgements

My Thanks to Karen Seek who read my manuscript to check that it was sound according to the Scriptures.

My Thanks to Pauline Hague, my niece who edited, copy –edited and put my manuscript into word soft.

My Thanks to my granddaughter Miriam Winkler who was my liason between my publisher and me.

I could not have published this book without the help from these dedicated ladies who I am blessed to have in my life.

Preface

There is no such thing as an ordinary life. To
say this would insult our Creator who values
every person who has ever lived, is living or
will live. He risked everything He is by giving
His life [1] to restore us to His own image. It
is a joy and privilege to walk with God day by
day. There is so much to discover about His
character; each day is full of surprises. Even
though I am now in my tenth decade I feel I
am hardly on the threshold of discovering the
immensity of who God is.

To discover anything for the first time is to be
overwhelmed with the feeling of wonder. Even a
child, however young, is capable of this incredible
feeling. For example, I well remember the
expression of utter delight and amazement when
our two year old son saw the ocean for the very
first time. The joy of his discovery was infectious

and I too was caught up in the rapture of what lay before me.

With this in mind, in some small way I seek to capture or recapture the joy of discovery. The physical realm alone delights us in countless ways by looking, listening, tasting, smelling and touching. Even the very act of taking one breath is enough to make you gasp with wonder. All of these fade in comparison with the pure delight of being able to communicate with our Maker.

Often times as I walk, I just have to stop and gaze at a snowdrop, violet or buttercup. These joys alone would fill volumes, but it is my personal discoveries as I have walked with God these past ninety years which I desire to share with you. As you read, my prayer is that you may take an inventory of your own gold and find joy in sharing it with others. Surely the old hymn expresses this with the opening words:

> I've found the pearl of greatest price
> My heart must sing for joy.
> And sing I must for Christ I have,
> Oh, what a Christ have I ? [2]

I have purposely not quoted the scriptures; instead I leave the references so you may find out the nuggets for yourself. Come with me and look into my treasure chest.

[1] John 3:16   [2] Redemption Songs No 159

Table of Contents

Introduction   *"My Mother Lode"*   *xvii*

Portion 1   *Surprise*   *1*

Portion 2   *A Useful Mistake*   *3*

Portion 3   *Guesstimates*   *7*

Portion 4   *Jehovah Jireh*   *9*

Portion 5   *Master*   *11*

Portion 6   *Fear*   *15*

Portion 7   *Fault Lines*   *19*

Portion 8   *The Secret*   *21*

Portion 9   *Anchoria*   *25*

Portion 10   *Altar of Exchange*   *29*

Portion 11   *Wine Skins*   *33*

Portion 12   *White Elephant*   *35*

Portion 13   *The Apple of His Eye*   *37*

Portion 14   *Clinging*   *41*

Portion 15   *Staked Out*   *43*

Portion 16   *The Common Herd*   *45*

Portion 17   *Rereward*   *49*

Portion 18   *$25 an Ounce*   *51*

Portion 19   *The Sharks*   *57*

Portion 20   *Inexhaustible*   *59*

INTRODUCTION

"My Mother Lode"

Any gold miner will tell you that nothing can compare with the thrill of first discovering his 'mother-lode' (a principal vein or zone of veins of gold ore); it is stamped indelibly in his heart and mind. It is now seventy six years since I discovered my 'mother-lode' and the memory is as fresh today as if it was but yesterday. This 'mother-lode' is burnished bright and will never lose its luster. All the fires on earth or in hell can never take away or reduce its value; it is truly indestructible.

I did not acquire this 'mother-lode' through any effort of my own; my sin and darkness were too deep for me to penetrate. For this to be accomplished it took Almighty God, in the form of His only Son to come to this earth and tunnel through every sin and darkness, as He gave His life blood on the cross.[3] Thus He made the way for everyone to become rich beyond their wildest dreams.

I am just a mere mortal coming from a very normal family background. No great fanfare announced my birth; nevertheless I always had a sense of security by being loved by my family. As a child I attended Sunday School, but found it boring. My formal education ended when I was fourteen and I began my first full time job at a wholesale newsagent.

It is quite normal for teenagers to want to break free from parental restrictions and I was no exception. I felt something was waiting to satisfy an inner craving. I had already decided not to attend church on a regular basis. I was looking for life and did not believe I would find it in church. The truth is, I didn't really know for what I was searching, but 'Someone' placed that yearning deep within me and only He could end my search and give me purpose.

In the year 1928 the Welsh evangelists Stephen and George Jeffreys came to the nearby town of Doncaster to hold revival meetings. These were days before television and not everyone had a radio. Consequently news of these meetings did not reach our village, even though it was only three miles away. In those days that was considered quite a distance!

Nevertheless those meetings made a tremendous impact on hundreds of people. The churches became alive with vibrant worship. Of course, I knew nothing of these happenings, being only nine years old at the time; I doubt if my parents were even aware, either. Some revivals have been known to fizzle out after a while, but not this one. Five years later I was to discover the truth of this in a very real way.

One of mother's work colleagues, Annie Pullen, was known for her solemn disposition and didn't endear herself to people. This changed one day, prompting my mother to become curious as to what had caused this apparent change in her personality. Annie was only too delighted to enlighten my mother. She was one of many folk who had been to the revival meetings and responded to God's call. Her beaming countenance displayed her obvious transformation.

My mother had chosen to take a job at the suggestion of her doctor. He thought it might help her overcome her deep sorrow at the loss of her one and only baby son. My parents already had five daughters, so when our brother was born he brought great joy to my parents. Even after six years she still had a deep sense of loss.

Upon seeing the transformation in Annie's life, there was born in my mother's heart a desire to find a real peace, too. Annie was only too willing to share what God had done for her and invited my mother to go along with her to the church to hear the 'Good News' for herself.

Mother went along willingly; as a result she also was touched by the Savior and my, how it showed in the radiance on her face. Now at last we had our mother back with her ready smile and joyous laughter. Truly she was transformed and it showed in so many ways.

From then on her one aim was to take her girls
to hear the same Gospel which had transformed
her life. One of the things I remember was how
mother described those meetings. She would
talk about the wonderful singing and how people
hugged each other. Of course, all this was foreign
to me, certainly not my idea of church as I knew it.
I came to the conclusion everyone must be crazy
who went there!

Mother had already taken along some of my
sisters and now it was my turn. I jumped at the
chance for two reasons. Firstly, I could have a
rare trip into the town of Doncaster, which would
include an ice cream cone. Secondly, my main
reason was I simply thought this church had
people who were "off their heads", so as far as I
was concerned, I would have lots of fun from the
experience. So it was with a measure of curiosity I
first went to this "crazy" church.

I had no idea I was on the verge of discovering
my 'mother-lode'. On entering the church my
whole attitude changed completely. I expected
to laugh and ridicule, but no, the sense of the
presence of God was awesome; it truly felt like holy
ground.

Something was happening in the deepest
recesses of my heart, stirrings I had never known
before. As the service drew to a conclusion the
pastor gave an invitation to anyone who would like
to give their heart to Christ to raise a hand. At
this moment my heart was thumping in my chest
and tears were pouring down my face. Two main

streams of thoughts were going through my mind at the same time. Firstly, it was as if Christ was saying to me, "I love you so much that if you were the only person in the world I would still have given my life for you." Tears still fill my eyes every time I recall those tender moments.

Secondly, I felt I was at a crossroad. Either I was going to accept Christ or reject Him. It was at that crucial moment Mother looked down on my tear-stained face and asked me, "Do you want to raise your hand?" Without hesitation I nodded my head. How grateful I am to my mother for being sensitive to my need at that time. I just knew without a shadow of doubt I did not want to reject Christ but accept Him into my life.

It is now seventy six years since this happened to me but it is as vivid as if it had happened today. I can understand a little of what Jesus meant when He said, "You must be born again."[4] As a baby spends nine months in the darkness of the mother's womb before emerging into the light, so my spirit was in darkness until I came into God's glorious light.

It would be foolish to expect a baby to want to go back into its mother's womb after being in the light. I felt exactly the same from the very first day Christ came into my heart. From being a young teenager seeking to have a good time and looking for "I knew not what"; I knew I had found my "mother-lode".

As a result of this decision my whole life took on new meaning. Jesus Christ became real to me and I longed to lead others to know Him too. A consuming desire to read and study God's Word engulfed me; along with that came the desire to pray daily.

A new world opened up to me as I made friends with a large group of people, who like me, had recently come to know Christ. Since that time, like most people, my life has had its ups and downs, but one thing I have never doubted: God's Word is true when Jesus says, "I am with you always, even unto the end of the world." [5]

Most will have heard the phrase, "like father, like son". Jesus was the perfect portrayal of His Father. To know God we must look at Jesus. I understand from Scripture the purpose and intent of God's heart is to restore us to His own image and that image is presented to us through His own Son, Jesus Christ. [6] I know the plan and purpose of God is for us to take on the likeness or image of His Son. [7] This process takes a whole life time. When a baby is born it is often difficult to see any parental resemblance, but as the child matures, likenesses become more obvious.

I am sure that as our Heavenly Father looks down on us, His heart rejoices as He begins to see Christ being formed in us.[8] I pray that as you read these pages your heart will dance for joy at the recollection of your own personal 'mother-lode'. If perchance you have not yet discovered your personal 'mother-lode', it is right there in God's Word, [9] yours for the taking. God bless you.

No Name has meant so much to me
Oscar C. Eliason

I've learned to know a Name I highly treasure,
Oh how it thrills my spirit through and through.
Oh, precious Name, beyond degree or measure,
Oh wondrous Name of Him so kind and true.

That Name brings gladness to a soul in sorrow,
Ii makes life's shadows and its clouds depart;
Brings strength in weakness for today, tomorrow,
That Name brings healing to an aching heart.

That Name still lives and will live on forever,
While kings and kingdoms will forgotten be;
Thro' mist or rain, 'twill be beclouded never,
That Name will shine and shine eternally.

My heart is stirred whene'er I think of Jesus,
That blessed Name which sets the captive free;
The only Name thro' which I find salvation,
No Name on earth has meant so much to me.

[3] Philippians 2 : 6-8   [4] John 3 : 3   [5] Matt. 28 : 20 (KJV)   [6] Heb. 1 : 3
[7] Rom. 8 : 29   [8] Gal. 4 : 19   [9] Matt. 13 : 34

PORTION 1

Surprise

From my store of bright shining nuggets I am going to let you share my latest one at the time of writing. My granddaughter Lois and her husband live in Louisville, where they attend a mega church. On my last visit my great granddaughter, Johnnie Elyse invited me to go with her to the Youth Service. There is a great difference between a ninety year old and someone who is seventeen. I felt very honored that Johnnie would even ask me and of course I said," Yes".

I had never been to a young people's meeting since my own early days. I know things have changed a great deal over the years, so I went to the meeting with the same attitude I had when I first found my 'mother-lode', one of curiosity and expecting a laugh and a giggle.

It seems history has a way of repeating itself. As on my first occasion I was filled with surprise

and awe as I watched the vast number of teenagers
being caught up in rapturous worship of God. Yes,
at times the music was loud, very loud and then,
to my great surprise, a switch as they began to
sing, "Let the beauty of Jesus be seen in me". This
was a song I first heard just after I came to Christ.
Immediately this took my mind back in time,
seventy six years, to that very moment when Christ
entered my heart.

Now came the time for us to take of the bread
and wine in remembrance of the Lord's death.
By now my whole spirit was overwhelmed with the
sweet presence of Almighty God. With bowed head
I held the bread and wine. For a few precious
moments I had a very real sense that Jesus Himself
was standing there giving me the bread and the
wine, reminding me again that had I been the only
person in the world, He would have died for me,
so great is His love. Indeed this was a very precious
moment for me.

I know that in God's eyes it is alright for
a ninety year old to worship Him alongside
teenagers. God doesn't see age groups; He only
sees His children.

PORTION 2

A Useful Mistake

"Gran'ma, I've arranged for you to give the weekly devotion at Ellie Joy's school next week." The voice came from my youngest granddaughter, Miriam, with whom I was visiting in South Carolina a short while ago. Sounds reasonable, but when you consider it must have been at least sixty years since I addressed children of combined ages; I had every reason to feel a little trepidation.

However, it would never occur to me to say "No" to Miriam. My book "Tales from the Teapot" had been published recently so it was expected that I would give the devotion from the book. Let me explain. In writing about tea I discovered some parts of the tea story could be used to give spiritual lessons. After much thought and prayer I prepared the ten minute talk for the eight to eight thirty devotion. How was I going to get my point over clearly in just ten minutes and at such an unearthly hour?

This was to be the very first time I had ever spoken to school children; I had spoken to children in Sunday School, but this was somewhat different, more regimental. Sure enough, on the stroke of eight, every child from the first to the seventh grades trooped into the chapel, looking resplendent in school uniform. The big school clock stared at me as I rose to speak at 8:15. It seemed to shout at me, "8:25, 8:25, don't go past me!"

"Camellia Sinensis, Triune God." These were the four words I called out to my audience. This had the effect of grabbing their attention. I would try and help them understand their meaning. I illustrated these words with the use of props. I had a leafy branch which I placed in water. This was to represent the bush, Camellia Sinensis. I placed a brown earthenware teapot by the side to represent earth. Then I began to explain how Camellia Sinensis was like the Triune God, one in three and three in one,[10] God the Father, the Son and the Holy Spirit. Just as Camellia Sinensis is made up of branches, leaves and water, the Triune God is one in three and three in one.

I took a leaf from the branch and placed it in the brown earthenware teapot. This told us how Jesus, the Son, willingly left His Father and came down to earth to live among us.[11] Something happened while Jesus was on earth. He died on a cross for the sins of the whole world.[12] Before

He died He told the disciples He would rise from the dead, go back to His Father and send the Holy Spirit to earth so that all who come to Him would have eternal life.[13]

As I related this truth to the children I lifted the teapot lid, pulled out a tea bag and took it back to the branch to tie it on, so now we have Jesus back in heaven with the Father just as He said.

But there is more. Did He not say He would send the Holy Spirit? Yes indeed, as I talked, gently I took the water supporting the branch and began to pour it into the earthenware teapot explaining that was like the promised Holy Spirit being poured into the world.

Still something else is needed. I picked up what I thought was a child's brown teacup, explaining that we must receive Christ into our hearts through the Holy Spirit. As I poured, simultaneously a low giggle began and I was conscious of a dribbling on my foot. In a moment the words came to me, "Yes, that is what God wants to do in our lives; He pours His spirit in, so we can pour out to others." Let me explain the dribble. I had been looking for a play teacup and by mistake I had picked up a play plant pot with a hole in the bottom.

Perhaps you may be wondering why I find this episode to be a nugget of gold. It shines brightly to me for several reasons, one being, with God's help I was able to get my points across on time. That big school clock seemed to smile at me at 8 : 35 a.m. Secondly I am so grateful the Lord gave me just the right words to say when the dribble began. The teacher assured me that was one lesson the children would not forget.

Thirdly, I was greatly blessed as I realized that even though it is difficult to visualize God, the Scriptures say no man has seen God at any time, yet unmistakably, Jesus is God manifest in the flesh and Heaven is where Jesus is now. So undeniably when I go to Heaven and see Jesus I will be looking on God Himself.

My last words to the children were, "Triune God, Camellia Sinensis, just forget them; just simply say, Jesus, tea. All we need to do is enjoy."

[10] Eph. 1 : 17 [11] John 1 : 14 [12] Rom. 5 : 8 [13] John 16 : 5-13

PORTION 3

Guesstimates

There are human footprints on the moon. It was a truly memorable day when they were first planted there. In a recent quiz game we were asked to give an estimate of how many years it will take before those footprints will disappear. Needless to say, all our answers were greatly underestimated. The number left me breathless; it might as well have been never. The reason: there is no wind on the moon.

This caused me to think of how the Son of God came to this earth. His footprints were left in such a way that it is impossible to remove them. I speak of the impact He has had and will continue to have in this world of ours. There has never been and never will be anyone whose mark and influence have so much power to change lives. The footprints of Jesus can be seen today in countless numbers of lives. I am so pleased He placed His footprints on my life.[14]

Thank you Kristen and Porter for introducing me to the game, Guesstimates.

[14] Col. 1 21-23

PORTION 4

Jehovah Jireh

Many people know that Jehovah Jireh means
"The Lord will provide", but despite this I believe
there are many people who worry about their future
provision. I was one of those people. When my
husband and I were buying our first house I had a
secret worry as to how we would be able to keep up
our monthly payments if our circumstances should
change.

God has His own ways of putting our fears at
rest. My husband and I always loved to attend the
National Girls Choir whenever they performed in
our home town. On one of those occasions the girl
soprano, who usually sang the solo parts, was absent.
A girl with a contralto voice replaced her. The title
of one of her songs grabbed my attention. "God
will provide" were the heart piercing words which
filled my ears.

This thought enveloped me: the God who loves me is the God who[15] provides. From that moment on I ceased to worry; He certainly did provide and continues to do so. Sometimes I wonder why it takes some of us so long before we really learn to trust Him. Jesus had so much to say about us trusting our Heavenly Father.

A little baby is born into this world trusting in mother. When we are born into God's family why do some of us worry about our daily needs? "Do not worry"[16] I was so grateful to leave behind the worry I had carried. Unfortunately, life has a way of bringing other things into our lives which can cause us to worry and fret about them.

I wish I could say this lesson had taught me what to do about every concern and care which would ever come my way. That was not the case. I would pray, yes, but still walk away carrying the load I intended leaving with a loving Heavenly Father. I have made significant progress even though I had to reach my ninth decade before I finally found the large nugget of really trusting God. I will now proceed to tell you of my great discovery.

[15] Gen. 22 : 14   [16] Luke 12 : 22 - 25

PORTION 5

Master

It does not take us very long to realize that many situations arise which are completely out of our control. In such times we feel vulnerable and are tempted to worry, especially when our loved ones are involved. One such situation occurred when I was in my mid forties. I began to feel anxious, and my anxiety increased as I did not have anyone with whom I could share my concern.

Oh yes, I prayed earnestly about the situation and despite this I still carried the anxiety away with me. Then one day, in the darkness I could see a glimmer of gold shining brightly before me. It seemed as if Christ Himself asked me the question, "Am I the Master?" My heart leaped with hope and joy. Here at last was the key. All this time

I had not been trusting Him and I hadn't even realized it.

I left God's presence fully confident that if He, the Almighty, is in control, there is nothing to fear. Did a miracle occur right away? No, indeed not, in fact, for a while the situation grew even worse. Did my anxiety return? No. Through it all I knew everything was in His hands; it seemed as if I heard the constant whisper, "Remember, I am the Master."

The Master did not leave me wondering about the final outcome for too long. I can tell you the whole situation completely turned around, which was beyond anything I could have envisaged. Yes, yes, yes, He still does far more than we can ask or think. At long last I am so grateful to have discovered this priceless nugget of gold.

[17] 1 John 2 : 1

Part 2

Several years ago a loved one found himself in a serious predicament without any hope of a solution. Naturally I was concerned and began to pray earnestly about the situation. I knew I really trusted in God even though I could not see any way out. On one particular day, as I was in prayer, The Lord came to me again with the distinct message, "I am the Master". How gracious is our God that He deigns to let us know His intentions. I was filled with a deep peace, certainty and joy, knowing that all would be well.

I told my loved one I was certain that despite the outward dismal signs the Master would work it out. Shortly afterwards everyone was amazed when the whole situation was turned around for good. Who better can we have as our advocate than the Lord of Glory, the Creator of the universe? If only I had learned the secret years ago, the sweet word, "Master".

Part 3

You would think by now I would have it altogether as far as worrying is concerned. No, everything has to be practiced. It reminds me of playing scales on the piano, every scale is in a different key.

Several years ago, for the first time in my life I was faced with a serious financial crisis which was completely out of my control. At the same time I was having health problems which didn't help at all. I must confess to being truly stressed out; I was in strange territory. How patient is God with us. At last He caught my attention with the very same words, "Am I your Master?" Again I felt the overwhelming sense of peace, joy and assurance flowing over my soul. Once more God demonstrated His awesome power in the way the financial mess was resolved. When He speaks, things happen.

Part 4

Today, as I begin my ninety second year the question could be asked, "Am I completely free of

worry?" The answer is yes and no. Each day I take
a lot of medication, because of certain physical
weaknesses. If I take my medication regularly I am
well but if I neglect it, I suffer the consequences.
That is how I view my tendency to worry over
things. While ever I focus on the Master I do not
worry, but if I fail to focus on Him I am beset with
anxiety and care. Many things have happened
since I believed Jesus to be my Master; by the
grace of God, I have learned to cast all my cares
upon Him.[18] Life now takes on a new meaning.
There can be a sense of adventure and relish when
things go awry sometimes. My heart can be filled
with anticipation as to how the Master is going to
demonstrate His might and authority.

I have found there are great benefits from
truly knowing and believing that Christ is Master.
I attribute my health and well-being to being
worry-free. You can be a great encourager to many
people around who are struggling and worrying.
Jesus had much to say to us about not worrying[19], so
it must be an important lesson we need to learn
and practice daily.

---

[18] Matt. 8 : 27   [19] 1 Peter 5 : 7

PORTION 6

Fear

It is quite normal to feel fearful. A healthy fear
prevents us from doing foolish and irrational
things. People who demonstrate particular acts
of bravery in the face of extreme danger do so,
not because they are unafraid, but because their
courage overcomes their fear. These people are
both brave and rare.

There is such a thing as irrational fear and
I have possessed this fear on two occasions.
Although I did not recognize it at the time, I was
having a panic attack. When war was declared
between England and Germany in 1939 I was a
twenty year old. Three days after the declaration
we were awakened by the piercing sounds of sirens
warning us of an imminent air raid. Fear swept
over me, the like of which I had never known
before. No one else in the family seemed unduly
disturbed. I don't see the need to describe in

detail how it affected me, except to say it lasted
several days. Now I realize I had experienced a
major panic attack.

Where was my trust in God at that time? It
was simply not there. Incidentally, there was no
air-raid that night; it proved to be a flock of geese
flying overhead. Even that did not allay my fears.

Sixty six years later I had another panic
attack. This happened whilst taking care of my
two year old great granddaughter, Ellie Joy. As
I was changing her into her bedtime clothes she
grabbed the dusting powder and put it into her
mouth as toddlers are prone to do.

After I had taken her up to bed I began to
tidy up; I paused when I picked up the dusting
powder and began to read its label. I was horrified
to discover this powder was toxic. Waves of fear
overwhelmed me and I began to panic believing that
Ellie Joy was going to die and it would be my fault.
To say I was distraught would be an understatement.

I had to get help quickly and in my panic I
called Ellie's daddy to come home right away. By
now I was almost incoherent. Chris tried to assure
me that Ellie Joy was perfectly alright and Miriam
was soon on the scene. She did not seem to be
perturbed either and tried to reassure me.

I made my way up to bed, still in a state of panic
at what might have been. Unless you have had
a panic attack you cannot conceive the torture it
brings. After a while I seemed to sense in my spirit
God's word saying, "Perfect love casts out fear"[20].
It was then I realized my love is not perfect, God's

love is perfect and His is the love which casts out fear. Billowing waves of comprehension flooded over me and within seconds I was perfectly whole. Only God can do this. This is one lesson I will never forget. Since then I have had other opportunities to test my reaction to fear, but by the grace of God I lay hold of His Word, "perfect love casts out fear".

Occasionally my son and his wife go away for a day or so and on these occasions I would go and stay with family or friends because I was afraid to stay in the house alone. I realized I needed to put this fear to rest, so, to my family's surprise I told them I had decided to stay home the next time they were away.

My family assured me if I felt afraid they would be over to get me. It was a step of faith on my part and I looked forward in anticipation. As I knelt by my bedside I duly asked the Lord to protect the house and give me sound sleep. I did not have any fear at all but enjoyed a special sense of the presence of God. I needed to get up once or twice in the night and the same presence enveloped me. I even tried to ask myself, "Are you not a tiny bit nervous?" The answer was an emphatic, "No!"

How good is our God; we really do not have anything to fear. Every moment of our lives He is there. I am eternally grateful the Lord has delivered me from fear, both real and irrational. This bright nugget of gold will shine brightly in any dark tunnel you and I may be called to go through; it will never lose its luster.

[20] 1 John 4 : 18

Fault Lines

The earth's crust covers up many fault lines but
some are visible. These can serve as a warning of
impending disaster, as happened in the ancient
city of Sardis. It stood on a high rock, apparently
impenetrable for centuries. King Croesus had
become so confident in the invincibility of the city;
he assigned only a few soldiers to guard the walls.

One night the ever-watchful enemy observed a
guard accidentally drop his helmet over the wall.
As they watched, the guard climbed down the rock
face to retrieve his helmet. This led the enemy to
believe there must be a narrow fissure in the wall.
It did not take long for the unsuspecting city to
be taken captive by the use of the unguarded fault
line.

[21]We all have fault lines, some recognizable and
some hidden. Some we were born with; some are
of our own choosing. What we do with these fault

lines in our make-up is very important. Already I
am aware of some of mine; in times past they have
given me pain. For years I believed the enemy's lie
that I was made that way. Yes, I was born with those
fault lines, but God has shown me how to be on
my guard constantly by using the powerful Word
of the living God.[22] Our adversary, the devil, never
ceases to look for a loophole to enter our lives and
bring us into bondage.[23]

It is a great joy and comfort to know we are not
left vulnerable to every attack, in whatever form
it may come, but by faith we can give the safe-
keeping of our hearts to the mighty conqueror.
[24] That conqueror is Jesus Christ the Lord, who
already has rendered our enemy powerless.[25] I
like the opening lines of the hymn, "A mighty
fortress is our God".[26] I am delighted that at last I
can go to sleep each night, wake up each new day,
knowing my whole being, frail though it may be,
fraught with fault lines, is heavily guarded by the
commander of the whole universe. This is more
than sufficient to put the enemy into swift retreat.

[21] Psalm 51   [22] Eph. 6 : 17   [23] 1 Pet. 5 : 8   [24] Col. 2 :15

[25] A Mighty Fortress is Our God attr. to Martin Luther   [26] Psalm 46 : 1-2

PORTION 8

The Secret

How do you define the word, 'secret'? It is
something you know that no one else knows; then
you share your secret with someone else and it is
no longer a secret! For me the word has an air
of mystery about it, which automatically arouses
curiosity. Some people cherish a secret ingredient
they use in a particular recipe when cooking
a dish which is the envy of other cooks. They
are most reticent to give away the secret. Some
people are secretive by nature; I am quite the
opposite!

I have been considered old in years for quite
some time, but God has blessed me so that people
are amazed by my appearance and frequently ask
me, "What is your secret?" A straight question
requires a straight answer and I am always happy to
oblige. My answer is always the same, word by word:

"God keeps those young whom age doth chill,
whom God finds young He'll keep young still".
This answer seems to leave most people temporarily
puzzled.

It gives me great joy to explain the conundrum.
The first part, "God keeps those young whom age
doth chill", I explain like this: [27]When a person
takes God into his life, automatically the life of
God through His Spirit indwells them. This life is
eternal life and even when our body shows signs of
decay this life of God still throbs within.

The second part of the saying, "whom He finds
young He'll keep young still" has particular relevance
to me as I was young when Christ entered into my
life. This has many advantages; not only are you
saved from many pitfalls but you have a lifetime to
learn how to trust Him fully when faced with 'trials
and tribulations'.

The conclusion I have come to when explaining
the secret of how I look is quite simple: at last I
have ceased to struggle. Instead, I give each day to
a loving Heavenly Father. Yes, [28]relinquishment is
the secret to a peaceful, happy life. I have a great
peace within, knowing that whatever each day
brings, it is God who is the director. Even though I
may not see what is ahead, my part is simply to trust
Him.

Is there any wonder that my blood pressure
is that of a twenty year old? After years of
dangerously erratic readings I am delighted at
this amazing improvement. I am so grateful to

know the One who came to give us life and that more abundantly. [29] Certainly this eternal life has a beneficial effect on our mortal bodies.

[27] 1 John 4 :15   [28] Rom. 12 : 1-2   [29] John 10 : 10

PORTION 9

Anchoria

One of my favorite hymns contains the line, "We have an anchor that keeps the soul". It carries with it a sense of security and solidarity. It has always conjured up in my mind a picture of a boat on a storm-tossed sea. Its only hope of survival was when the anchor was cast into the sea to fasten itself onto a seabed rock.

Recently I came upon the word "Anchoria". As I read I was delighted to gain greater insight. Here we have a picture of a boat, anticipating the oncoming storm, anchoring in the harbor. Instead of dropping the anchor over the side of the boat and hoping for the best, the sailors took advantage of the "anchoria".

The "anchoria" was a huge rock located on the shore. To become anchored to this rock a sailor would secure a long rope to the boat and with the

other end tied around him, he would jump into
the turbulent sea and swim to shore. Once there
he would fasten the rope to the rock securely. The
sailors left behind on the storm-tossed boat would
wait in hope for the first tug of the rope, assuring
them that now they were well and truly anchored.
Gone were the fears of ever becoming adrift or
wrecked, however long the storm would rage.

A vivid picture filled my mind as I began to
think of how Jesus has been with us in the boat of
this world.[30] He bridged the gap between us and
God by plunging into death, coming through every
obstacle to reconcile us to God. This is described
in the scripture[31] which says we have a fore-runner,
Jesus, who has entered into God's presence on
our behalf. As Jesus has gone before, now we can
be safely connected to Him. When difficult times
come we can feel the tug between us and our
"anchoria", giving us the assurance "we have an
anchor that keeps the soul steadfast and sure as
the billows roll: fastened to the Rock which cannot
move grounded firm and deep in the Savior's
love".

As we anchor in life's harbor, we can feel the
gentle tug of the rope, which assures us of God's
presence whether our lives are going through
turbulence or tranquility. Peace, security,
confidence; what more do we need? I am so glad
to be firmly anchored to the solid rock. If you
have not yet taken hold of the rope of security
God is offering you, I urge you to grasp hold of
it by faith. You will feel its gentle pull when the

storms of life threaten. You will experience God's assurance continually. Then you will be able to sing with the hymn writer, "It is well, it is well with my soul".

[30] John 1 : 10 [31] Heb. 6 : 19-20

PORTION 10

Altar of Exchange

I believe most evangelical Christians are familiar
with the phrase, "an altar call". I have no idea
when this phrase was first used, howbeit, I know
an 'altar call' is an invitation given at the end of a
service to anyone who desires to receive Christ's
offer of salvation or to rededicate themselves
afresh to Christ. Altars were used thousands of
years ago to make sacrifices, mostly of animals and
even live humans. These sacrifices were a means
of appeasing the gods of different cultures and to
curry favor.

Almighty God used the altar of sacrifice to
demonstrate His passionate desire for sinful man
to have communion with Himself. Each year
God required the sins of His people to be placed
upon an animal free from any blemishes and then
sacrificed before Him. This was to be a picture
of His one and only Son, who at the appointed

time was to come to earth, live a pure, blameless
life before giving Himself as a living sacrifice[32] for
the sins of the whole world, as He went to the cross
to die. This sacrifice was final and did not need to
be repeated.

Why do I write all this? It is one of my favorite
nuggets of gold brought to me unexpectedly by my
friend Karen Seek. She told how the minister at
the Brooklyn Tabernacle Choir had explained that
the altar was much more than a place of sacrifice;
it was also a place of exchange. Immediately I
understood what he meant. Under the old system
sacrifices were made repeatedly, without any
lasting benefit. How different was the ultimate
sacrifice which God made on our behalf!

Now as we come to the altar of exchange we
are rich beyond measure. Our first and foremost
exchange comes when we approach the cross and
lay all our sins on the One who has paid in full
the demands of a righteous and holy God. Then
we take from Him the robe of righteousness to
wear continually.[33] Free at last, the burden of
our past sin has been forgiven and we are clean
through Him.

There are many other things we can exchange
at the cross. We are called to bring all our
weaknesses, whatever they may be and exchange
them for God's enabling power to overcome them
through the Holy Spirit dwelling within us. We
can bring to Him our daily needs, whether they are
financial or otherwise and lay those cares upon the
altar, taking up the promise of His provision.

Many of us grieve over loved ones who seem to be going astray. Come, lay down your deep concerns and take away the blessed assurance that He is able to keep that which you have committed to Him. There is a vast gold mine for you to take, just come as you are, leave everything you have and are at the cross, make the great exchange today; there is no time like now; do not delay, I pray.

[32] John 1 : 29   [33] 1 Cor. 1 : 30

PORTION 11

Wineskins

For years the phrase "new wine in new bottles" puzzled me. This changed on the first Sunday of 2011 when our pastor began to explain the true meaning behind it. In Bible times wine was stored not in bottles but in wineskins. Sometimes empty wineskins were left lying around and as a consequence they would become hard and brittle and hence unsuitable for holding new wine.

A wineskin could be restored for its original purpose by being submerged under running water for many hours, which caused the skin to become pliable again and free from cracks. Our pastor explained how the word, 'new' when referring to wineskins does not mean 'new' but 'restored' or 'renewed'. When I heard this I considered it to be another bright nugget of gold I had discovered that day, as I considered what Jesus was implying in the parable He had taught.[34]

Wineskins had one purpose, to hold new wine.
In the beginning God created us for one purpose,
so that we may be filled with God Himself and
have communion with Him. Without the presence
of God in our lives we become dried up, cracked
and useless and not what God intended us to be.
However, there is a way to be restored. God has
provided the constant washing in the water of His
Word and as we yield ourselves to Him daily, we
find our dryness becoming softened as we become
pliable in the Master's hands. [35]

Can you not feel the throb of excitement as
you contemplate the possibilities there are for you
if you would be willing to yield your dry, cracked
self to the gentle wooing of the Holy Spirit? He
wants to restore and transform you into what
God intended for you. I know what it means to
have the washing of His Word through His Spirit
and to feel the daily renewal of God's indwelling
presence.

Life takes on an entirely new meaning when we
quit hanging around becoming drier and crustier.
God has so much more to offer than that. New
wine in new bottles; what could sound better than
that? It is your choice: dry and crusty or sparkling
and life giving!

[34] Mark 2 : 18-22   [35] 2 Cor. 3 : 18

PORTION 12

White Elephant

"White Elephant" is a well known phrase, but where did it come from? Like me, you may have not given it much thought, just assuming it referred to something you had been given and didn't really want. Recently I came across the true story which explains this phrase.

It is recorded that the King of Siam had a special tactic for defeating his enemy. He would give him the sacred gift of a white elephant. This elephant was never put to work and was expensive to keep as it would consume vast amounts of food. This tactic weakened the enemy because the elephant required time, energy and expense. I can well imagine the enemy feeling flattered when first receiving such a gift, but then he would realize he had been hoodwinked.

This story caused me to see how easy it is for those who walk with God to be deceived by their enemy, to allow his "white elephants" to enter into their lives. The "white elephant" is unprofitable and time consuming. The main lesson I learned from this is to be most careful what I allow into my life, especially those time consuming things which detract from my walk with the Lord. How many of us have fallen prey to accepting a "white elephant" into our lives? If we are serious about walking with God, we will be on guard against anything which will cause our time, energy and resources to drain away, leaving us less effective as Christians.

Fundraisers often have "White Elephant" stalls where people are given the opportunity of donating those "white elephants" as a way of ridding themselves of them.[37] But this takes courage! As we walk with God we too have the choice to rid ourselves of all those unprofitable things in our lives so we can choose a better way.

[36] Word for Today 1-04-2011   [37] Heb. 12 : 1

PORTION 13

The Apple of His Eye

I imagine most English speaking people have heard
or even used the expression, "the apple of his eye".
Its use goes back thousands of years, even mentioned
in the Old Testament. Nowadays this idiom is used
figuratively to describe something, or more usually
someone, cherished above others. When I think
of it, an apple, however attractive, seems a poor
description of someone or something we treasure,
but we have grown to understand and accept its
meaning.

Several years I ago I found an entirely new
meaning of this phrase. The scripture in Psalm 17 :
8 became alive and vibrant. I discovered the word
"apple" should have been translated "pupil". This
made much more sense to me. As I began to
ponder the implications of being the pupil of God's
eye I received greater understanding. So vividly it
portrays how precious we are in God's sight.

He will do everything necessary to guard and protect His children. In Deuteronomy 32 : 10 He declares He will guard us as He guards His own eyes. In Proverbs 7 : 2 He declares we are of great value. In Zechariah 2 : 8 He declares He will take revenge on anyone who hurts us. What a legacy for the child of God to know that every moment, whether sleeping or waking, we are never out of the personal care of the living God, who holds us so dear to His heart.

Have you ever pondered what it must be like to live in darkness because the pupils of your eyes don't function? It's hard to imagine not seeing the smile of a child or the rising and setting of the sun, just two examples of the millions of beautiful things our Creator has given us. This causes me to remember the time in my life when I was blind to the things of God, until my spiritual eyes were opened and I was able to have a personal relationship with Him. As I value the pupils of my physical eyes, so in a greater way I value and guard my spiritual pupils, which keep me in constant communication with the Living God. Now all God's creation appears even more beautiful than it did before, as expressed in the refrain of an old hymn:

Loved With Everlasting Love

Heav'n above is softer blue,
Earth around is sweeter green;
Something lives in every hue
Christless eyes have never seen:
Birds with gladder songs o'erflow,
Flowers with deeper beauties shine,
Since I know, as now I know,
I am His and He is mine.
Since I know, as now I know,
I am His and He is mine.

G. Wade Robinson.

PORTION 14

Clinging

"I was tired of waiting so I left" is a familiar saying, the key word being "tired". How does that fit in with the familiar and well-loved scripture in the Bible,[38] "They that wait upon the Lord shall renew their strength"? It sounds like a contradiction.

Try waiting for a bus that does not turn up or a flight which is cancelled suddenly. How do you feel when someone is incredibly late for dinner and then appears without even an apology? Do we become strong while waiting?

One day I heard the explanation of the term "wait on the Lord". I read that the word "wait", in this particular context, means to twine around as a vine twines around a tree. How my heart was filled with joy and light at this revelation.

As I pondered, I began to see that as the vine needs the support of a strong tree to thrive so I, in my weakness and frailty, need to wrap myself around Almighty God. He is the one who is strong enough to give me support and be my strength from day to day, enabling me to flourish.

This gold nugget is most precious to me day by day, as I entrust my whole life to Him. I pray that you too will come and entwine yourself around the Lord.

[38] Isaiah 40 : 31

PORTION 15

Staked Out

Our breath came in gasps as we struggled valiantly down to the beach, battling against the strong gusty wind. We were anticipating long blissful hours just relaxing peacefully, but the sharp cut of the sand in our faces told us this would be unlikely, unless we remedied the dismal situation.

Before I realized what was happening, my granddaughter, Alecia had procured the service of a beach attendant to erect a wind-barrier. I watched with fascination as he secured the wind breaker with great dexterity. For many hours we were able to enjoy the sunshine in a restful and relaxing manner, knowing we were well and truly staked out.

[39]Isaiah 26 : 3 tells us: "Thou wilt keep him in perfect peace whose mind is stayed on Thee because he trusteth in Thee." The people of Isaiah's day would be able to picture a nomad sitting peacefully at the entrance to his tent, knowing that

it was firmly staked and secured in the sand. Should a sudden sand storm erupt, his sense of safety would not diminish, as he made his way into his tent until the storm passed over.

What a beautiful illustration this is of the peace and security we have when our whole lives are entrusted to the living God. To me, "stayed" gives the feeling of permanence and firmness. Yes, the sands of time and circumstances are shifting constantly but we can say with the apostle Paul,[40] "He is able to keep that which I have committed to Him against that day". What are the stakes which keep us grounded so well? They are nothing less than the multitude of promises which we find in God's Holy Word.

So, let the winds of adversity throw at us what they may; we have nothing to fear as we are firmly staked out and grounded firm and deep in the infallible promises of God.

[39] KJV   [40] 2 Tim. 1 : 12

PORTION 16

The Common Herd

In medieval England, the 'common' played an essential part in village life. Let me explain. A common is a piece of open land belonging to all members of a community. It was used by individuals to graze their animals for as long as they wanted. Occasionally an animal was barred from the others by means of a barrier, possibly because it was sick or the owner feared for its safety. Common ground still exists in England but in these days of modern farming methods, animals are rarely seen grazing on village commons.

Many years ago I came across the ancient meaning of the word 'fellowship'. It literally means, 'the common herd', or could it refer to the herd which grazes on the common as they were 'in fellowship'? As for the animal separated from the others by a barrier, he would be 'out of fellowship'. Sometimes the barrier would be lifted then he would be 'back in fellowship' or 'back with the common herd'.

In today's usage, the phrase 'the common herd' has acquired a derisory meaning and I don't think that connotation may go away. As I discovered this nugget of information my heart leaped at the significance of the word 'fellowship'. We have common ground in the assurance of salvation as [41]'whosoever' may come and graze.

The Lord has not erected any barriers to exclude anyone from his offer of salvation. The common ground on which we stand is the same for rich or poor, or any other comparison you care to make. I don't know of anything else in the world which comes close to the fellowship we find being with God's children.

Sometimes we can put a barrier around ourselves. I've heard some say they don't need to go to church; they can worship without other people. Maybe there is a barrier of unconfessed sin. Whatever barrier we have erected it is time to get into fellowship again. We have heard the words, 'out of fellowship'; this is very sad.

Without a doubt we know it is the Lord's prayer and desire that His children should be one in fellowship just as Jesus is one with the Father.[42] To be in fellowship is to bring joy to the Father's heart. Surely we all need the fellowship of each other for our personal development and encouragement.

I could not visualize a life without the fellowship of my brothers and sisters in Christ; my life is enriched beyond measure because of it. May you, too, come to value that which has been freely made available to you, through the price Christ paid to purchase the 'common land', so you may be part of the 'common herd'.

[41] John 3 : 16   [42] John 17 :10-23

Rereward

When I became a Christian as a young teenager, I was encouraged to read the Bible. In those days most Christians read the King James Version, often referred to as the 'Authorized Version of the Holy Bible'. This version of the Bible is 400 years old and it was written in the language of that age. Consequently it contains words which are archaic and therefore never heard nowadays. One of these words is 'rereward'. In Isaiah 58 : 8[43] it says: 'Then shall thy light break forth as the morning, and thine health shall spring forth speedily: and thy righteousness shall go before thee; and the glory of the LORD shall be thy rereward.'

In recent years we have numerous modern versions of the Bible and in most of these the word 'rereward' is replaced by 'rear guard'. This gives the picture of troops who protect the rear of a military formation. In the dictionary we can find the word 'rearward' which is similar to the older word 'rereward' and this means 'in the rear or towards the rear'.

I was at a Bible study with Beth Moore when she shed a different light on the same scripture in Isaiah 58. When contemplating the meaning of the words 'that the glory of the LORD shall be your rereward' Beth drew a picture of a farmer sowing seeds and a long way behind was the reaper gathering up the harvest. Evidently the word 'rereward' comes from a Hebrew word which has several meanings, one of which was 'to gather in' or 'to harvest'. To see this scripture in this light is to bring hope and encouragement as we sow seeds daily for God's Kingdom, possibly without ever seeing the results.

Who could have envisioned the mighty harvest Billy Graham was to reap when as a young teenager he received God's Word into his heart, as Mordecai Ham faithfully sowed the seed in his congregation?

Perhaps we do not fully realize how much seed we are sowing as we journey through life, but one day we may be surprised when the Great Reaper reveals to us the results of our sowing. Our task is to sow; it is the Lord who gives the increase, but He needs faithful sowers. Will you be one?

[43] K.J.V. Isaiah 58 : 8

PORTION 18

$25.00 an ounce

I watched with curiosity as our hostess, Jeannie prepared tea. Long ago I gave up the fallacy that only the English know how to make tea. It was quite normal to expect the usual cups, saucers, sandwiches, fancy cakes, pristine tablecloth and suchlike to appear. However, our conversation ceased as Jeannie entered the room, placing on the table a small round tray about nine inches in diameter and about 2½ inches deep. Inside was a very small teapot; surrounding this were nine tiny cups without handles. You would hardly give them a second glance as they were of a dull grey color and void of any tasteful decoration. Jeannie proceeded to pour hot water over the whole thing, filling both teapot and cups.

Then she entered the room with a small packet of tea, approximately two ounces in weight. On opening the packet I was given a peek inside. At

first glance what I saw appeared to be dark raisins.
I held my breath as Jeannie informed us of the cost
of this small packet. $50.00!

At this moment our attention was riveted on
every single move that Jeannie made. Three
pieces of tea were dropped into the very hot
teapot, then boiling water was poured in and the
lid replaced. After a minute or so Jeannie handed
a cup to each of us, then she began to pour out
the tea. As she did so I could see it was almost
void of color. Simultaneously we lifted our cups to
our lips not knowing what to expect. Oh surprise,
surprise! My taste buds responded with sheer
delight. Could this taste be as near as one could
get to having tea made from freshly picked leaves
from the Camellia Sinensis tree?

We continued drinking from the same pot of
tea for several rounds as Jeannie kept refilling it
with boiling water. Strange as it may sound, the
strength of the tea did not diminish but grew
stronger, leaving an indescribable taste in my
mouth for quite some time.

When we had finally finished, Jeannie plucked
a piece of tea from the teapot. To my amazement
I saw a dark green stem with its topmost leaf and
the tiny leaves just below. I have no idea how
the tea was processed to retain its character as if
freshly picked, but it made me realize this would
be how it was marketed centuries ago. The tea we
drink today bears little resemblance to the tea I
tasted that night with my friends.

This experience helped me to discover a new nugget of gold. I pray that as I try to explain you will make the nugget your very own. It was because this experience was not what I had anticipated, it caught my attention. It reminded me of the many times God has moved in my life unexpectedly.

When making a cup of tea, many of us have fixed ideas as to how it should be done. It would appear many of us have a similar attitude when considering how we should worship God. Some people are concerned more about how we worship God, using ritual, places and special forms of music, rather than who we worship.

Several years ago an English worship leader came to this very same realization. For several weeks the church put aside the musical instruments, which had played a key part in their worship; instead they were totally focused on the Lord. This resulted in the congregation gaining a new awareness of intimacy with God. From this powerful experience the worship leader was inspired to write the beautiful song, "I'm coming back to the heart of worship". The Samaritan woman at the well was given the very same message from Jesus when He said, "They that worship me must worship me in Spirit and truth."[44]

While pondering about my delightful tea experience I began to see that I am like a simple earthenware teapot. The astonishing discovery is that Christ desires to dwell in me through the Holy Spirit.[45] As I peeked into the small teapot after we had finished, I noticed the tea had so expanded after the boiling water was added, that it had filled the teapot. This reminded me of Ephesians 1 : 23,[46] Colossians 1 : 19[47] and Colossians 2 : 9[48] which declare that all the fullness of God dwells in Christ. The whole universe is filled with His glory. How wonderful to know that we only have to stretch out our cup to Him and He is only too willing to fill us up again and again.

Well might the prophet Isaiah call out, "Come ye to the waters and drink".[49] The beautiful words of Jesus say it all in John 7 : 37 "If any man thirst let him come to me and drink."[50]

Jesus seems to show His glory quite unexpectedly. The three disciples will never forget the moments of the transfiguration of Jesus.[51] We have the two disciples on the road to Emmaus.[52] Their world had seemingly come to an end with the death of Jesus, when behold, Jesus Himself drew near. How the heart of Mary Magdalene leapt for joy when she heard the Master's voice near the garden tomb.[53]

He appears to those who do not know Him and even persecute Him. Read how His voice arrested Saul of Tarsus, resulting in his life being completely turned around and him becoming Paul the Apostle.[54] The Master is still speaking to us today.[55] Each time the memory of the moment is etched deep within us forever. My prayer is that we all may continue to find joy and surprise as we journey through life with Him.

[44] John 4 : 24   [45] Col. 1 : 27   [46] Eph. 1 : 23   [47] Col. 1 : 19   [48] Col. 2 : 9

[49] Isa. 55 : 1   [50] John 7 : 3   [51] Mark 9 : 2   [52] Luke 24 : 15   [53] John 20 : 10

[54] Acts 9 : 4   [55] John 14 : 21

PORTION 19

The Sharks

He stood all alone, as he waited with baited breath before the panel of 'sharks' debating their final offer for his invention. "The Sharks" is not my phrase but the name of the television show I was watching. They made it abundantly clear their sole purpose was to make money and plenty of it.

Finally the suspense was over for the tremulous young man as he awaited their offer. He was told, in no uncertain terms, they deemed him incapable of handling big business. Like a bolt from the blue they offered to buy him out completely, including the right to patent his invention. Thus he would walk away, stripped of all he had worked for, but an exceedingly wealthy man.

He stood quietly for several seconds then in a clear decisive voice said, "No thank you, gentlemen" and with head held high, turned around and walked away. I saw a man who would

not barter that which he held most dear in
exchange for financial security. Here was a man
to be admired indeed.

Clearly this was one huge nugget of gold to me,
as in my mind's eye I saw the Savior walking away
from all the blandishments of the devil, who tried
everything to thwart His purpose of being here to
bring redemption to mankind.

This incident has meaning for us today. Our
soul is the most valuable thing we possess. Satan
is always on the prowl, dangling all kinds of
temptations before us to draw us away from our
true purpose in life. Jesus gave the warning,
"What shall it profit a man, if he gains the whole
world, and lose his own soul? Or what shall a man
give in exchange for his soul?" Mark 8 : 36-37

It took great courage for the young man
to reject the lucrative offer from the 'Sharks'.
Sometimes we may be called upon to decide
between worldly fame or wealth and the well-being
of our soul.

Beverley Shea, also known as 'The Beloved
Gospel Singer', knew what it was to turn his back
on a promising singing career to devote his life
to singing the gospel. The song, "I'd rather have
Jesus" by Rhea F. Miller became his signature
song.

> *I'd rather have Jesus than men's applause.*
> *I'd rather be faithful to His dear cause.*
> *I'd rather have Jesus than worldwide fame.*
> *I'd rather be true to His Holy Name.*

PORTION 20

Inexhaustible

Desolate, deserted, derelict, a deathly pall hangs over the once prosperous gold mine, which once rang with jocund laughter of gold miners flushed with success. Relics of the past lie rusting; now all is barren and still.

This is not a picture of the gold mine of my life. My finds, rather than declining, have increased in size and number. The air seems filled with the gold dust representing the vast number of the promises of God. God's Word speaks of "the unsearchable riches of Christ" Ephesians 3 : 8. Truly "no eye has seen, no ear has heard, no mind has conceived what God has prepared for those who love him." 1 Corinthians 2 : 9 and yet there is more!

I pray as you travel through life you will be blessed as you discover your very own mother-lode and enjoy the unearthing of endless nuggets of gold. The joy will never end but rather increase as you look forward in anticipation to reaching the source itself, the very heart of the Living God.

Psalm 145 : 3 "Great is the Lord and most worthy of praise; His greatness no one can fathom."

Scripture References

1. John 3 : 16
2. Redemption Songs No. 159
3. Philippians 2 : 6-8
4. John 3 : 3
5. Matthew 28 : 20
6. Hebrews 1 : 3
7. Romans 8 : 29
8. Galatians 4 : 19
9. Matthew 13 : 34
10. Ephesians 1 : 17
11. John 1 : 14
12. Romans 5 : 8
13. John 16 : 5-13
14. Colossians 1 : 21-23
15. Genesis 22 : 14
16. Luke 12 : 22-25
17. 1 John 2 : 1
18. Matthew 8 : 27
19. 1 Peter 5 : 7
20. 1 John 4 : 18
21. Psalm 51
22. Ephesians 6 :17
23. 1 Peter 5 : 8
24. Colossians 2 : 15
25. A Mighty Fortress is Our God Attributed to Martin Luther.
26. Psalm 46 : 1-2
27. 1 John 4 : 15
28. Romans 12 : 1-2
29. John 10 : 10
30. John 1 : 10
31. Hebrews 6 : 19-20
32. John 1 : 29
33. 1 Corinthians 1 : 30
34. Mark 2 : 18-22
35. 2 Corinthians 3 : 18
36. Word for Today 1 - 4 - 11
37. Hebrews 12 : 1

38. Isaiah 40 : 31
39. Isaiah 26 : 3 K. J. V.
40. 2 Timothy 1 : 12
41. John 3 : 16
42. John 17 : 10-23
43. Isaiah 58 : 8
44. John 4 : 24
45. Colossians 1 : 27
46. Ephesians 1 : 23

47. Colossians 1 : 19
48. Colossians 2 : 9
49. Isaiah 55 : 1
50. John 7 : 37
51. Mark 8 : 2
52. Luke 24 : 13
53. John 20 : 10
54. Acts 9 : 4
55. John 14 : 21